This book belongs to:

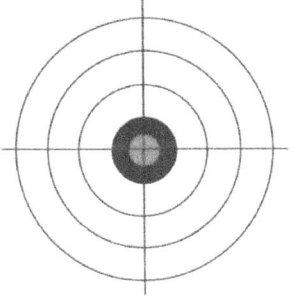

Date					
Location					
Time	AM/PM	Hunting Partner(s)			
Weather conditions					

Terrain

Time	Species	Size	Seen	Shot	Lost	Captured

Wildlife Sightings

Gear/Set Up

Notes

Date				
Location				
Time	AM/PM	Hunting Partner(s)		
		Weather conditions		
		Terrain		

Time	Species	Size	Seen	Shot	Lost	Captured

Wildlife Sightings

Gear/Set Up

Notes

Date			
Location			
Time	AM/PM	Hunting Partner(s)	
		Weather conditions	

Terrain

Time	Species	Size	Seen	Shot	Lost	Cap-tured

Wildlife Sightings

Gear/Set Up

Notes

Date			
Location			
Time	AM/PM	Hunting Partner(s)	
		Weather conditions	
		Terrain	

Time	Species	Size	Seen	Shot	Lost	Captured

Wildlife Sightings

Gear/Set Up

Notes

Date				
Location				
Time	AM/PM	Hunting Partner(s)		
		Weather conditions		
		Terrain		

Time	Species	Size	Seen	Shot	Lost	Cap-tured

Wildlife Sightings

Gear/Set Up

Notes

Date			
Location			
Time	AM/PM	Hunting Partner(s)	
		Weather conditions	

Terrain

Time	Species	Size	Seen	Shot	Lost	Captured

Wildlife Sightings

Gear/Set Up

Notes

Date				
Location				
Time	AM/PM	Hunting Partner(s)		
		Weather conditions		

Terrain

Time	Species	Size	Seen	Shot	Lost	Cap-tured

Wildlife Sightings

Gear/Set Up

Notes

Date						
Location						
Time	AM/PM	Hunting Partner(s)				
Weather conditions						
Terrain						

Time	Species	Size	Seen	Shot	Lost	Captured

Wildlife Sightings

Gear/Set Up

Notes

Date				
Location				
Time	AM/PM	Hunting Partner(s)		
Weather conditions				

Terrain

Time	Species	Size	Seen	Shot	Lost	Captured

Wildlife Sightings

Gear/Set Up

Notes

Date				
Location				
Time	AM/PM	Hunting Partner(s)		
		Weather conditions		
		Terrain		

Time	Species	Size	Seen	Shot	Lost	Captured

Wildlife Sightings

Gear/Set Up

Notes

Date				
Location				
Time	AM/PM	Hunting Partner(s)		
Weather conditions				

Terrain

Time	Species	Size	Seen	Shot	Lost	Cap-tured

Wildlife Sightings

Gear/Set Up

Notes

Date							
Location							
Time	AM/PM	Hunting Partner(s)					
		Weather conditions					
		Terrain					

Time	Species	Size	Seen	Shot	Lost	Captured

Wildlife Sightings

Gear/Set Up

Notes

Date					
Location					
Time	AM/PM	Hunting Partner(s)			
		Weather conditions			
		Terrain			

Time	Species	Size	Seen	Shot	Lost	Captured

Wildlife Sightings

Gear/Set Up

Notes

Date				
Location				
Time	AM/PM	Hunting Partner(s)		
		Weather conditions		

Terrain

Time	Species	Size	Seen	Shot	Lost	Captured

Wildlife Sightings

Gear/Set Up

Notes

Date				
Location				
Time	AM/PM	Hunting Partner(s)		
		Weather conditions		

Terrain

Time	Species	Size	Seen	Shot	Lost	Captured

Wildlife Sightings

Gear/Set Up

Notes

Date				
Location				
Time	AM/PM	Hunting Partner(s)		
		Weather conditions		

Terrain

Time	Species	Size	Seen	Shot	Lost	Captured

Wildlife Sightings

Gear/Set Up

Notes

Date				
Location				
Time	AM/PM	Hunting Partner(s)		
		Weather conditions		

Terrain

Time	Species	Size	Seen	Shot	Lost	Captured

Wildlife Sightings

Gear/Set Up

Notes

Date					
Location					
Time	AM/PM	Hunting Partner(s)			
		Weather conditions			
		Terrain			

Time	Species	Size	Seen	Shot	Lost	Cap-tured

Wildlife Sightings

Gear/Set Up

Notes

Date				
Location				
Time	AM/PM	Hunting Partner(s)		
Weather conditions				

Terrain

Time	Species	Size	Seen	Shot	Lost	Captured

Wildlife Sightings

Gear/Set Up

Notes

Date			
Location			
Time	AM/PM	Hunting Partner(s)	
		Weather conditions	

Terrain

Time	Species	Size	Seen	Shot	Lost	Captured

Wildlife Sightings

Gear/Set Up

Notes

Date				
Location				
Time	AM/PM	Hunting Partner(s)		
Weather conditions				

Terrain

Time	Species	Size	Seen	Shot	Lost	Cap-tured

Wildlife Sightings

Gear/Set Up

Notes

Date				
Location				
Time	AM/PM	Hunting Partner(s)		
		Weather conditions		
		Terrain		

Time	Species	Size	Seen	Shot	Lost	Captured

Wildlife Sightings

Gear/Set Up

Notes

Date			
Location			
Time	AM/PM	Hunting Partner(s)	
Weather conditions			

Terrain

Time	Species	Size	Seen	Shot	Lost	Captured

Wildlife Sightings

Gear/Set Up

Notes

Date			
Location			
Time	AM/PM	Hunting Partner(s)	

Weather conditions

Terrain

Time	Species	Size	Seen	Shot	Lost	Captured

Wildlife Sightings

Gear/Set Up

Notes

Date				
Location				
Time	AM/PM	Hunting Partner(s)		
		Weather conditions		

Terrain

Time	Species	Size	Seen	Shot	Lost	Captured

Wildlife Sightings

Gear/Set Up

Notes

Date				
Location				
Time	AM/PM	Hunting Partner(s)		
Weather conditions				

Terrain

Time	Species	Size	Seen	Shot	Lost	Captured

Wildlife Sightings

Gear/Set Up

Notes

Date				
Location				
Time	AM/PM	Hunting Partner(s)		
		Weather conditions		

Terrain

Time	Species	Size	Seen	Shot	Lost	Captured

Wildlife Sightings

Gear/Set Up

Notes

Date				
Location				
Time	AM/PM	Hunting Partner(s)		
		Weather conditions		

Terrain

Time	Species	Size	Seen	Shot	Lost	Captured

Wildlife Sightings

Gear/Set Up

Notes

Date			
Location			
Time	AM/PM	Hunting Partner(s)	
		Weather conditions	

Terrain

Time	Species	Size	Seen	Shot	Lost	Captured

Wildlife Sightings

Gear/Set Up

Notes

Date			
Location			
Time	AM/PM	Hunting Partner(s)	
		Weather conditions	
		Terrain	

Time	Species	Size	Seen	Shot	Lost	Captured

Wildlife Sightings

Gear/Set Up

Notes

Date					
Location					
Time		AM/PM	Hunting Partner(s)		
			Weather conditions		

Terrain

Time	Species	Size	Seen	Shot	Lost	Captured

Wildlife Sightings

Gear/Set Up

Notes

Date				
Location				
Time	AM/PM	Hunting Partner(s)		
		Weather conditions		

Terrain

Time	Species	Size	Seen	Shot	Lost	Cap-tured

Wildlife Sightings

Gear/Set Up

Notes

Date				
Location				
Time	AM/PM	Hunting Partner(s)		
		Weather conditions		

Terrain

Time	Species	Size	Seen	Shot	Lost	Cap-tured

Wildlife Sightings

Gear/Set Up

Notes

Date				
Location				
Time	AM/PM	Hunting Partner(s)		

Weather conditions

Terrain

Time	Species	Size	Seen	Shot	Lost	Captured

Wildlife Sightings

Gear/Set Up

Notes

Date				
Location				
Time	AM/PM	Hunting Partner(s)		
Weather conditions				

Terrain

Time	Species	Size	Seen	Shot	Lost	Captured

Wildlife Sightings

Gear/Set Up

Notes

Date				
Location				
Time	AM/PM	Hunting Partner(s)		
Weather conditions				

Terrain

Time	Species	Size	Seen	Shot	Lost	Captured

Wildlife Sightings

Gear/Set Up

Notes

Date				
Location				
Time	AM/PM	Hunting Partner(s)		
Weather conditions				

Terrain

Time	Species	Size	Seen	Shot	Lost	Cap-tured

Wildlife Sightings

Gear/Set Up

Notes

Date				
Location				
Time	AM/PM	Hunting Partner(s)		
Weather conditions				

Terrain

Time	Species	Size	Seen	Shot	Lost	Captured

Wildlife Sightings

Gear/Set Up

Notes

Date				
Location				
Time	AM/PM	Hunting Partner(s)		
Weather conditions				

Terrain

Time	Species	Size	Seen	Shot	Lost	Captured

Wildlife Sightings

Gear/Set Up

Notes

Date				
Location				
Time	AM/PM	Hunting Partner(s)		
		Weather conditions		
		Terrain		

Time	Species	Size	Seen	Shot	Lost	Captured

Wildlife Sightings

Gear/Set Up

Notes

Date				
Location				
Time	AM/PM	Hunting Partner(s)		
		Weather conditions		

Terrain

Time	Species	Size	Seen	Shot	Lost	Cap-tured

Wildlife Sightings

Gear/Set Up

Notes

Date				
Location				
Time	AM/PM	Hunting Partner(s)		
		Weather conditions		
		Terrain		

Time	Species	Size	Seen	Shot	Lost	Captured

Wildlife Sightings

Gear/Set Up

Notes

Date				
Location				
Time	AM/PM	Hunting Partner(s)		
Weather conditions				

Terrain

Time	Species	Size	Seen	Shot	Lost	Captured

Wildlife Sightings

Gear/Set Up

Notes

Date						
Location						
Time	AM/PM	Hunting Partner(s)				
		Weather conditions				
		Terrain				

Time	Species	Size	Seen	Shot	Lost	Captured

Wildlife Sightings

Gear/Set Up

Notes

Date				
Location				
Time	AM/PM	Hunting Partner(s)		
		Weather conditions		
		Terrain		

Time	Species	Size	Seen	Shot	Lost	Cap-tured

Wildlife Sightings

Gear/Set Up

Notes

Date			
Location			
Time	AM/PM	Hunting Partner(s)	
		Weather conditions	

Terrain

Time	Species	Size	Seen	Shot	Lost	Captured

Wildlife Sightings

Gear/Set Up

Notes

Date			
Location			
Time	AM/PM	Hunting Partner(s)	
		Weather conditions	

Terrain

Time	Species	Size	Seen	Shot	Lost	Captured

Wildlife Sightings

Gear/Set Up

Notes

Date				
Location				
Time	AM/PM	Hunting Partner(s)		
		Weather conditions		
		Terrain		

Time	Species	Size	Seen	Shot	Lost	Captured

Wildlife Sightings

Gear/Set Up

Notes

Date				
Location				
Time	AM/PM	Hunting Partner(s)		
Weather conditions				

Terrain

Time	Species	Size	Seen	Shot	Lost	Captured

Wildlife Sightings

Gear/Set Up

Notes

Date				
Location				
Time	AM/PM	Hunting Partner(s)		
Weather conditions				

Terrain

Time	Species	Size	Seen	Shot	Lost	Captured

Wildlife Sightings

Gear/Set Up

Notes

Date				
Location				
Time	AM/PM	Hunting Partner(s)		
Weather conditions				

Terrain

Time	Species	Size	Seen	Shot	Lost	Captured

Wildlife Sightings

Gear/Set Up

Notes

Date						
Location						
Time	AM/PM	Hunting Partner(s)				
Weather conditions						

Terrain

Time	Species	Size	Seen	Shot	Lost	Captured

Wildlife Sightings

Gear/Set Up

Notes

Date					
Location					
Time		AM/PM	Hunting Partner(s)		
			Weather conditions		

Terrain

Time	Species	Size	Seen	Shot	Lost	Cap-tured

Wildlife Sightings

Gear/Set Up

Notes

Date						
Location						
Time	AM/PM	Hunting Partner(s)				
Weather conditions						
Terrain						

Time	Species	Size	Seen	Shot	Lost	Captured

Wildlife Sightings

Gear/Set Up

Notes

Date			
Location			
Time	AM/PM	Hunting Partner(s)	
		Weather conditions	

Terrain

Time	Species	Size	Seen	Shot	Lost	Captured

Wildlife Sightings

Gear/Set Up

Notes

Notes

Notes

Notes

Notes

Notes

Notes

Notes

Notes

Notes

Made in the USA
Monee, IL
08 December 2021